Post-Truth Picture Book

"The very concept of objective truth is fading out of the world."
George Orwell

Post-Truth Picture Book
by Donna J. Roberts

© 2017 Donna J. Roberts

Outside The Lines Press

www.outsidethelinespress.com

ALL RIGHTS RESERVED

ISBN: 978-0-9949240-7-0

This book contains material protected under International and Federal Copyright Laws and Treaties. Any unauthorized reprint or use of this material is prohibited. No part of this book may be reproduced or transmitted in any form or by any means, electronic or mechanical, including photocopying, recording, or by any information storage and retrieval system without express written permission from the author / publisher.

 Outside the Lines Press

Cat

Chair

Trumpet

Bread

Horse

Truck

House

Train

Puppy

Cow

Flower

Banana

Lion

Shoe

Owl

Hat

Fish

Frog

Tree

Juice

Pencil

Table

Baby

Snake

Bubble

Fork

Bear

Foot

Tiger

More fun and funny books from Outside the Lines Press

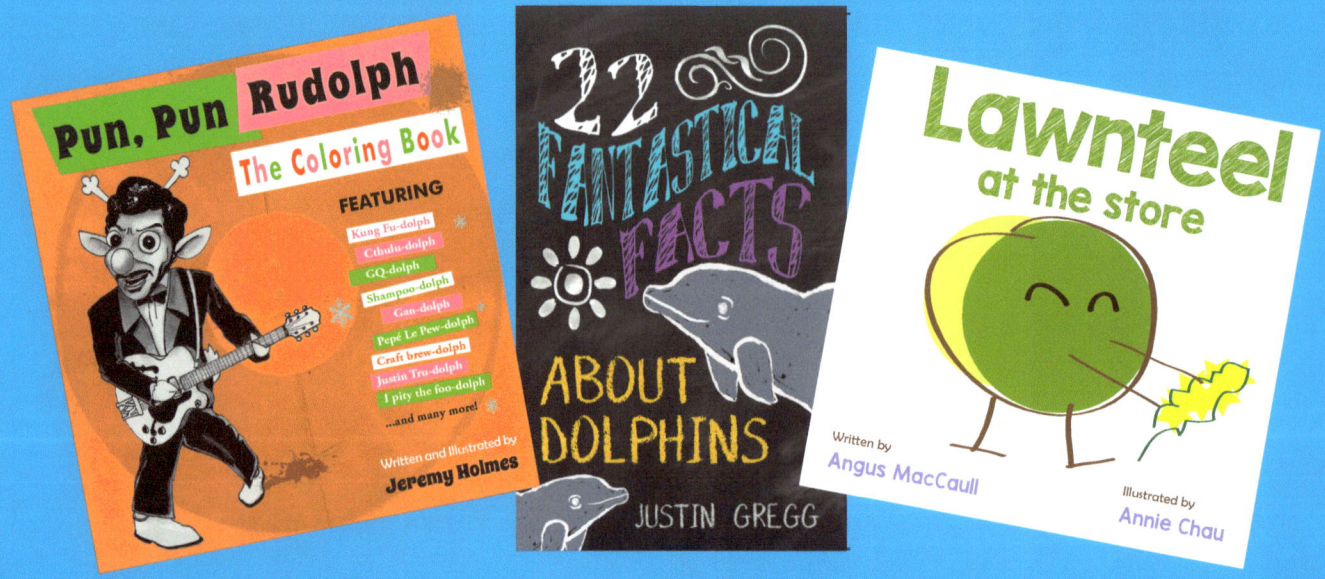

www.outsidethelinespress.com

Outside the Lines Press